Betty Crocker's *1-2-3* Dinner

350 Quick and Delicious Supper Solutions

Library of Congress Cataloging-in-Publication Data

Crocker, Betty.
    Betty Crocker's 1-2-3 dinner : 350 quick and delicious supper solutions.
        p.   cm.
    Includes index.
    ISBN 1–57954–523–8   hardcover
    1. Suppers.   2. Quick and easy cookery.   I. Title: 1-2-3 dinner.   II. Title: Betty Crocker's one-two-three dinner.
III. Title.
TX738 .C76   2001
641.5'55—dc21   2001004477

GENERAL MILLS, INC.
Betty Crocker Kitchens
Manager, Publishing: Lois Tlusty
Recipe Development: Betty Crocker Kitchens Home Economists
Food Stylists: Betty Crocker Kitchens Food Stylists
Photography: Photographic Services Department

Cover and Interior Design: Joanna Williams

10 9 8 7 6 5 4 3 2   hardcover

Cover: Ginger Couscous with Apple, page 136

For more great ideas visit www.bettycrocker.com.

Contents

Introduction

Beat the boring dinner blues with *Betty Crocker's 1-2-3 Dinner*! Turn to Betty Crocker for simple solutions—America's favorite cook is at your side. With *Betty Crocker's 1-2-3 Dinner*, you'll find all the answers to meet your quick cooking needs. The recipes are limited to three concise, easy-to-follow steps, so you won't find any elaborate or complicated techniques to follow. Check out the "Have a Minute?" and "Come and Eat!" tips with many recipes for ideas on how to make meal planning easy and fun.

Of course, the most rewarding part about cooking with *Betty Crocker's 1-2-3 Dinner* is the delicious taste! Even though these recipes cheat on time, they make up for it with big flavor. Who says short recipes mean bland meals? Not Betty Crocker. You'll find mouthwatering chicken, fish, beef and pork dishes—plus sensational soups, salads, pasta, pizza and more. Choose from homestyle favorites such as Chicken Stew over Biscuits or Meatballs and Mashed Potatoes. Or why not try something fun and new such as Thai Turkey Burrito Sandwiches, Polenta with Italian Vegetables or Pork Cutlets and Apple, Walnut and Gorgonzola Salsa? You'll love every bite of Linguine with Tuscan Vegetable Alfredo Sauce or Chicken Enchilada Pizzas.

Each recipe has been approved by the Betty Crocker Kitchens, so you can count on each dish tasting absolutely delicious.

Betty Crocker

Fix It Fast!

How can you get out of the kitchen faster? There are many easy ways to speed up preparation of ingredients and cooking. Some of our suggestions are listed here and you probably have some quick-cooking tricks up your sleeve as well. With a little planning and organizing, getting out of the kitchen faster will be simple.

Kitchen Tools—The Right Stuff

It's so true: The right tool for the right job does make your life easier. Timesaving kitchen tools are so helpful to have on hand. Consider some of our favorites:

- Apple wedger
- Self-cleaning garlic press
- Spring-loaded ice-cream/cookie scoops
- Egg slicer
- Fat separator
- Nonstick cookware
- Vegetable peeler
- Kitchen shears (regular and spring-loaded)
- Wire whisks
- Blender/food processor (large and mini)
- Hand mixer
- Microwave oven

Speedy Kitchen Secrets

Do you feel the need for speed? By learning a few techniques to cut corners, you will be a pro when it comes to cooking more quickly! Falling into the "why didn't I think of that?" category, these ideas couldn't be easier:

- Toss frozen or fresh vegetables into the pasta cooking water during the last few minutes of cooking. This is great for one-pan cleanup when making tossed pasta mixtures.

- It's the size that counts. For faster cooking, cut vegetables, meat and poultry into smaller or thinner pieces.

- Need boiling water in a hurry? Start with hot water and cover the saucepan with a lid; it will come to a boil faster.

- Speedier meat loaf can be made by pressing the uncooked meat loaf mixture into muffin tins instead of a loaf pan—you've just cut the baking time in half!

Do It Now, Save Time Later

As long as the cutting board or food processor is out, why not chop up another onion or two and pop them in a freezer bag for another time? Practically speaking, just taking that extra bit of time to prepare really saves you time in the future. And on one of those nights when you'd rather not cook and you're reaching into the freezer, you can thank yourself for thinking ahead! Check out these ideas:

- Chop onions, bell peppers, celery and carrots. Place desired amount in resealable plastic freezer bags or containers with lids, label and date. Freeze up to one month. To use, add directly to food being cooked without thawing.

- Form extra uncooked hamburger patties. Place waxed paper between the patties, wrap tightly, label and date. Freeze up to four months. To use patties, thaw before cooking.

- Cook ground beef and drain. Place desired amount in resealable plastic freezer bags or containers with lids, label and date. Freeze up to three months.

- Make extra meatballs, uncooked or cooked. Arrange meatballs in single layer on baking pan or cookie sheet; freeze. Remove meatballs from baking pan. Place desired amount in resealable plastic freezer bags or containers with lids, label and date. Freeze up to six months. Add cooked meatballs directly from freezer to food being cooked. If using uncooked meatballs, make certain to cook until meatballs are no longer pink in center and juice is clear.

Chicken Marsala (page 16)

Quick Chicken and Fish

Moroccan Spiced Chicken

Grilled Caribbean Jerk Chicken with Banana-Peach Chutney

4 servings

*Caribbean jerk seasoning includes red pepper, thyme and allspice all in one little jar!
The banana and peach stirred into prepared chutney add a fresh fruit flavor. This chicken can be broiled too.
Broil with top of chicken four to six inches away from heat for the same amount of time as in step 2.*

 2 tablespoons Caribbean jerk seasoning
 1 tablespoon vegetable oil
 2 tablespoons lime juice
 4 skinless, boneless chicken breast halves (about 1 pound)
 ½ cup chutney
 1 large banana, coarsely chopped
 1 large peach, chopped

Have a Minute?

Spread hot cooked rice on a serving platter and top with chicken and chutney. Garnish with grated lime peel and chopped peanuts.

1. Heat coals or gas grill. Mix jerk seasoning, oil and 1 tablespoon of the lime juice. Rub mixture on chicken.

2. Cover and grill chicken 4 to 6 inches from medium heat for 8 to 10 minutes, turning once, until juice is no longer pink when centers of thickest pieces are cut.

3. While chicken is grilling, mix chutney, banana, peach and remaining 1 tablespoon lime juice. Serve chicken with chutney.

1 Serving: Calories 225; Fat 7g; Cholesterol 60mg; Sodium 80mg; Carbohydrate 25g (Dietary Fiber 2g); Protein 25g.

Moroccan Spiced Chicken

4 servings

 1 tablespoon paprika
 ½ teaspoon salt
 ½ teaspoon ground cumin
 ¼ teaspoon ground allspice
 ¼ teaspoon ground cinnamon
 4 boneless, skinless chicken breast halves (about 1¼ pounds)
 1 tablespoon vegetable oil
 1 small papaya, sliced

1. Mix paprika, salt, cumin, allspice and cinnamon. Coat both sides of chicken with spice mixture.

2. Heat oil in 10-inch skillet over medium heat. Cook chicken in oil 15 to 20 minutes, turning once, until no longer pink when centers of thickest pieces are cut. Serve chicken with papaya.

1 Serving: Calories 195; Fat 8g; Cholesterol 75mg; Sodium 360mg; Carbohydrate 5g (Dietary Fiber 1g); Protein 27g.

Blackberry-Glazed Chicken
6 servings

½ cup blackberry jam
1 tablespoon Dijon mustard
6 boneless, skinless chicken breast halves (about 1¾ pounds)
1½ cups fresh or frozen (thawed, drained) blackberries

1. Brush grill rack with vegetable oil. Heat coals or gas grill for direct heat. Mix jam and mustard.

2. Cover and grill chicken 4 to 5 inches from medium heat for 10 minutes. Turn chicken; brush with jam mixture. Cover and grill 10 to 15 minutes longer or until juice of chicken is no longer pink when centers of thickest pieces are cut. Serve chicken topped with blackberries.

1 Serving: Calories 225; Fat 4g; Cholesterol 75mg; Sodium 110mg; Carbohydrate 22g (Dietary Fiber 2g); Protein 27g.

Grilled Lime Chicken Breasts
4 servings

¼ cup frozen (thawed) limeade concentrate
¼ cup vegetable oil
1 teaspoon finely shredded lime peel, if desired
¼ teaspoon paprika
4 boneless chicken breast halves (about 1 pound)

1. Heat coals or gas grill. Mix all ingredients except chicken.

2. Place chicken, skin sides up, on grill 4 to 6 inches from medium heat. Brush with limeade mixture.

3. Cover and grill 20 to 25 minutes, brushing frequently with limeade mixture and turning occasionally, until juice of chicken is no longer pink when centers of thickest pieces are cut. Discard any remaining limeade mixture.

1 Serving: Calories 285; Fat 21g; Cholesterol 60mg; Sodium 55mg; Carbohydrate 2g (Dietary Fiber 0g); Protein 22g.

Blackberry-Glazed Chicken

Skillet Chicken Parmigiana

Spicy Mexican Skillet Chicken

4 servings

Black beans can be hard to find. Sometimes they're shelved with other canned beans; they're often found with Mexican ingredients. If you can't find them in either location, kidney or pinto beans can be used instead.

1 to 2   **teaspoons chili powder**
  ¼   **teaspoon salt**
  ¼   **teaspoon pepper**
  4   **skinless, boneless chicken breast halves (about 1 pound)**
  1   **tablespoon vegetable oil**
  1   **can (15 ounces) black beans, rinsed and drained**
  1   **cup frozen whole kernel corn**
  ⅓   **cup thick-and-chunky salsa**
    Chopped fresh cilantro, if desired

Come and Eat!

Hot corn bread with a drizzle of honey is all that's needed to make this meal complete.

Have a Minute?

Sprinkle with cilantro and serve with lime wedges to squeeze on top.

1. Mix chili powder, salt and pepper. Sprinkle evenly over both sides of chicken breast halves.

2. Heat oil in 10-inch skillet over medium heat. Cook chicken in oil 8 to 10 minutes, turning once, until juice is no longer pink when centers of thickest pieces are cut.

3. Stir in beans, corn and salsa. Heat to boiling; reduce heat to low. Cover and simmer 3 to 5 minutes or until vegetables are hot. Sprinkle with cilantro.

1 Serving: Calories 304; Fat 7g; Cholesterol 60mg; Sodium 480mg; Carbohydrate 34g (Dietary Fiber 8g); Protein 34g.

Skillet Chicken Parmigiana

4 servings

  4   **boneless, skinless chicken breast halves (about 1¼ pounds)**
  ⅓   **cup Italian-style dry bread crumbs**
  ⅓   **cup grated Parmesan cheese**
  1   **egg, beaten**
  2   **tablespoons olive or vegetable oil**
  2   **cups spaghetti sauce**
  ½   **cup shredded mozzarella cheese (2 ounces)**

1. Flatten each chicken breast half to ¼-inch thickness between sheets of plastic wrap or waxed paper. Mix bread crumbs and Parmesan cheese. Dip chicken into egg, then coat with bread crumb mixture.

2. Heat oil in 12-inch skillet over medium heat. Cook chicken in oil 10 to 15 minutes, turning once, until juice is no longer pink when centers of thickest pieces are cut. Pour spaghetti sauce around chicken in saucepan; heat until hot. Sprinkle mozzarella cheese over chicken.

1 Serving: Calories 440; Fat 18g; Cholesterol 150mg; Sodium 980mg; Carbohydrate 31g (Dietary Fiber 2g); Protein 41g.

Southwest Chicken Skillet

4 servings

*Crush the tortilla chips neatly and easily by placing them in a heavy-duty plastic bag
and roll with a rolling pin until coarsely crushed.*

1 tablespoon vegetable oil
1 pound skinless, boneless chicken breast halves, cut into
   1-inch pieces
1 package (16 ounces) frozen corn, broccoli and red peppers
1 can (15 ounces) black beans, rinsed and drained
1 cup thick-and-chunky salsa
2 cups coarsely crushed tortilla chips
1 cup shredded Cheddar cheese (4 ounces)

1. Heat oil in 10-inch skillet over medium-high heat. Cook chicken in oil,
stirring occasionally, until brown.

2. Stir in vegetables, beans and salsa; reduce heat to medium. Cover and
cook 6 to 8 minutes, stirring occasionally, until vegetables are crisp-tender.

3. Sprinkle with tortilla chips and cheese. Cover and cook about 2 minutes or
until cheese is melted.

1 Serving: Calories 585; Fat 25; Cholesterol 90mg; Sodium 960mg; Carbohydrate 58g (Dietary Fiber 13g);
Protein 45g.

Come and Eat!

For a quick salad, top shredded lettuce with a scoop of guacamole and sprinkle with chopped tomato. Flan for dessert? Yes! Top servings of vanilla pudding with warmed caramel ice-cream topping and sprinkle with cinnamon.

Have a Minute?

Stir one small can of sliced ripe olives into the vegetable mixture in step 2.

Crispy Basil Chicken

6 servings

1/3 cup cholesterol-free egg product
2 tablespoons chicken broth
1 tablespoon Dijon mustard
1 clove garlic, finely chopped
1 1/2 cups dried bread crumbs
1 tablespoon dried basil leaves
1 teaspoon paprika
1/4 teaspoon white pepper
12 boneless, skinless chicken thighs (about 1 1/2 pounds)

1. Heat oven to 400°. Spray shallow roasting pan with nonstick cooking spray.

2. Mix egg product, broth, mustard and garlic in small bowl. Mix bread crumbs, basil,
paprika and white pepper in large plastic bag.

3. Dip chicken into egg mixture, then shake in bag to coat with crumb mixture. Place in
pan. Bake uncovered about 20 minutes or until juice is no longer pink when centers of
thickest pieces are cut.

1 Serving: Calories 305; Fat 10g; Cholesterol 95mg; Sodium 350mg; Carbohydrate 20g (Dietary Fiber 0g);
Protein 34g.

Quick Chicken with Olives and Tomatoes

6 servings

2 tablespoons margarine or butter

2 cloves garlic, crushed

1 small onion, chopped (about $\frac{1}{4}$ cup)

6 boneless, skinless chicken breast halves (about $1\frac{1}{2}$ pounds)

$\frac{1}{2}$ cup red wine vinegar

2 teaspoons chopped fresh or $\frac{1}{2}$ teaspoon dried thyme leaves

$\frac{1}{2}$ teaspoon salt

$\frac{1}{4}$ teaspoon pepper

2 large tomatoes, chopped (about 2 cups)

1 can ($2\frac{1}{4}$ ounces) sliced ripe olives, drained

1. Heat margarine in 10-inch skillet over medium-high heat until melted. Cook garlic, onion and chicken in margarine until chicken is brown on both sides.

2. Stir in remaining ingredients; reduce heat. Cook 10 to 15 minutes or until juice of chicken is no longer pink when centers of thickest pieces are cut.

1 Serving: Calories 200; Fat 8g; Cholesterol 65mg; Sodium 370mg; Carbohydrate 6g (Dietary Fiber 1g); Protein 27g.

Chicken Marsala

4 servings

    4   boneless, skinless chicken breast halves (about 1¼ pounds)
    ¼   cup all-purpose flour
    ¼   teaspoon salt
    ¼   teaspoon pepper
    2   tablespoons olive or vegetable oil
    2   cloves garlic, finely chopped
    ¼   cup chopped fresh parsley or 1 tablespoon dried parsley flakes
    1   cup sliced fresh mushrooms
    ½   cup dry Marsala wine or chicken broth

1. Flatten each chicken breast half to ¼-inch thickness between plastic wrap or waxed paper. Mix flour, salt and pepper. Coat chicken with flour mixture; shake off excess flour. Heat oil in 10-inch skillet over medium-high heat. Cook garlic and parsley in oil 5 minutes, stirring frequently.

2. Add chicken and brown each side. Add mushrooms and wine. Cook 8 to 10 minutes, turning once, or until chicken is no longer pink in center. Serve with hot cooked pasta if desired.

1 Serving: Calories 255; Fat 11g; Cholesterol 75mg; Sodium 220mg; Carbohydrate 11g (Dietary Fiber 1g); Protein 28g.

Easy Chicken Paprika

6 servings

    1   tablespoon vegetable oil
    6   boneless, skinless chicken breast halves (about 1½ pounds)
    1   large onion, sliced
  1½   cups milk
    2   tablespoons paprika
    1   can (10¾ ounces) condensed cream of chicken soup
    1   medium bell pepper, cut into strips
    4   cups hot cooked egg noodles

1. Heat oil in 10-inch skillet over medium heat until hot. Cook chicken and onion in oil, turning chicken once and stirring onion occasionally, until chicken is brown and onion is tender; drain.

2. Mix milk, paprika and soup; pour over chicken and onion. Stir in bell pepper. Heat to boiling, stirring occasionally; reduce heat.

3. Cover and simmer about 15 minutes or until juice of chicken is no longer pink when centers of thickest pieces are cut. Serve over noodles.

1 Serving: Calories 380; Fat 11g; Cholesterol 185mg; Sodium 660mg; Carbohydrate 37g (Dietary Fiber 1g); Protein 33g.

Chicken Marsala

Caesar Chicken with Orzo

Chicken and Mushrooms with Spaghetti

4 servings

4 boneless, skinless chicken breast halves (about 1 pound)
2 tablespoons olive or vegetable oil
2 cloves garlic, finely chopped
2 tablespoons finely chopped onion
1 cup sliced fresh mushrooms
1 medium green bell pepper, chopped (about 1 cup)
½ cup dry white wine or chicken broth
1 teaspoon red or white wine vinegar
1 jar (14 ounces) spaghetti sauce
   Hot cooked pasta, if desired

1. Flatten each chicken breast half to ¼-inch thickness between sheets of plastic wrap or waxed paper.

2. Heat oil in 10-inch skillet over medium-high heat. Cook garlic, onion, mushrooms and bell pepper in oil 5 minutes, stirring occasionally.

3. Add chicken to skillet. Cook about 8 minutes, turning once, until brown. Add wine and vinegar. Cook 3 minutes. Stir in spaghetti sauce. Cook 10 to 12 minutes or until juice of chicken is no longer pink when centers of thickest pieces are cut. Serve with pasta.

1 Serving: Calories 290; Fat 14g; Cholesterol 60mg; Sodium 810mg; Carbohydrate 14g (Dietary Fiber 1g); Protein 26g.

Caesar Chicken with Orzo

4 servings

1 tablespoon vegetable oil
4 boneless, skinless chicken breast halves (about 1¼ pounds)
1 can (14½ ounces) ready-to-serve chicken broth
1 cup water
1 cup uncooked rosamarina (orzo) pasta
1 bag (16 ounces) frozen broccoli, green beans, pearl onions and red peppers
3 tablespoons Caesar dressing
⅛ teaspoon coarsely ground pepper

1. Heat oil in 10-inch skillet over medium-high heat. Cook chicken in oil about 10 minutes, turning once, until brown. Remove chicken from skillet; keep warm.

2. Add broth and water to skillet; heat to boiling. Stir in pasta; heat to boiling. Cook uncovered 8 to 10 minutes, stirring occasionally, until pasta is tender. Stir in frozen vegetables (cut any large broccoli pieces in half) and dressing. Add chicken. Sprinkle with pepper.

3. Heat to boiling; reduce heat. Simmer uncovered about 5 minutes or until vegetables are crisp-tender and juice of chicken is no longer pink when centers of thickest pieces are cut.

1 Serving: Calories 370; Fat 13g; Cholesterol 70mg; Sodium 680mg; Carbohydrate 34g (Dietary Fiber 4g); Protein 33g.

Chicken Picante

4 servings

     2 **tablespoons margarine or butter**
     1 **pound skinless, boneless chicken breast halves, cut into 1-inch pieces**
     1 **medium zucchini, sliced (2 cups)**
     1 **cup sliced mushrooms (3 ounces)**
  2½ **cups picante sauce or salsa**
     2 **teaspoons sugar**

> #### Have a Minute?
>
> Make corn muffins using a package mix. Stir in ½ cup shredded sharp Cheddar or Monterey Jack cheese with jalapeño peppers into the batter.

1. Melt margarine in 10-inch skillet over medium heat. Cook chicken in margarine 4 minutes, stirring occasionally.

2. Stir in zucchini and mushrooms. Cook, stirring occasionally, until chicken is no longer pink in center and vegetables are tender.

3. Stir in picante sauce and sugar. Cook about 5 minutes, stirring occasionally, until hot.

1 Serving: Calories 230; Fat 9g; Cholesterol 60mg; Sodium 580mg; Carbohydrate 14g (Dietary Fiber 4g); Protein 27g.

Chicken with Garlic Bread Crumbs

4 servings

   ½ **cup seasoned dry bread crumbs**
   ¼ **cup chopped fresh parsley or 1 tablespoon parsley flakes**
   ¼ **teaspoon salt**
     2 **cloves garlic, finely chopped**
  1¼ **pounds boneless, skinless chicken breasts, cut into thin strips**
     1 **egg, beaten**
     2 **tablespoons margarine or butter**
        Spaghetti or barbecue sauce, warmed, if desired

1. Mix bread crumbs, parsley, salt and garlic. Dip chicken strips into egg, then coat with bread crumb mixture.

2. Melt margarine in 10-inch skillet over medium-high heat. Cook chicken in margarine 5 to 6 minutes, stirring occasionally, until no longer pink in center. Serve with spaghetti sauce.

1 Serving: Calories 265; Fat 9g; Cholesterol 140mg; Sodium 400mg; Carbohydrate 11g (Dietary Fiber 0g); Protein 35g.

Chicken with Garlic Bread Crumbs

Chicken and Apple-Rice Skillet

4 servings

 1 tablespoon margarine or butter
1¼ pounds boneless, skinless chicken breasts, cut into thin strips
 1 large unpeeled tart eating apple, sliced
1¾ cups chicken broth
 1 package (6.25 ounces) fast-cooking long grain and wild rice mix
   Additional apple slices, if desired

1. Melt margarine in 12-inch skillet over medium heat. Cook chicken and apple in margarine 10 to 12 minutes, stirring occasionally, until chicken is no longer pink in center.

2. Stir in broth and rice. Heat to boiling; reduce heat to low. Cover and simmer about 5 minutes or until rice is tender. Top with additional apple slices.

1 Serving: Calories 250; Fat 7g; Cholesterol 70mg; Sodium 560mg; Carbohydrate 20g (Dietary Fiber 2g); Protein 29g.

Chicken-Vegetable Couscous

6 servings

Couscous is a granular form of pasta, but is often used as a grain such as rice.
Couscous cooks in five minutes—perfect for meals when you are pressed for time.

 1 tablespoon olive or vegetable oil
 1 pound skinless, boneless chicken breast halves, cut into 1-inch pieces
 2 large tomatoes, chopped (2 cups)
 1 small red bell pepper, chopped (½ cup)
 8 medium green onions, chopped (½ cup)
 1 clove garlic, finely chopped
 1 tablespoon chopped fresh or 1 teaspoon dried oregano leaves
 1 teaspoon paprika
 1 can (15 to 16 ounces) garbanzo beans, rinsed and drained
 5 cups hot cooked couscous or rice
¼ cup grated Parmesan cheese

Come and Eat!

Serve with a crisp romaine lettuce salad tossed with ripe olives and Italian dressing.

1. Heat oil in 10-inch skillet over medium heat. Cook chicken in oil about 5 minutes, stirring occasionally.

2. Stir in remaining ingredients except couscous and cheese; cook 4 to 5 minutes or until vegetables are crisp-tender.

3. Serve over couscous. Sprinkle with cheese.

1 Serving: Calories 390; Fat 8g; Cholesterol 45mg; Sodium 610mg; Carbohydrate 57g (Dietary Fiber 7g); Protein 30g.

Chicken and Apple-Rice Skillet

Vegetable-Chicken Stir-Fry

4 servings

Stir-fry sauces are available in many varieties, from salty to sweet and mild to hot and spicy. Look for them in the Asian section of your supermarket.

- 2 **tablespoons vegetable oil**
- 1 **pound skinless, boneless chicken breast halves or thighs, cut into 1-inch pieces**
- 3 **cups cut-up assorted vegetables (bell peppers, broccoli flowerets, shredded carrots)**
- 1 **clove garlic, finely chopped**
- ½ **cup stir-fry sauce**

1. Heat 1 tablespoon of the oil in 12-inch skillet or wok over high heat. Add chicken, stir-fry about 3 minutes or until no longer pink in center. Remove from skillet.

2. Heat remaining 1 tablespoon oil in skillet. Add vegetables and garlic; stir-fry about 2 minutes or until vegetables are crisp-tender. Add chicken and stir-fry sauce. Cook and stir about 2 minutes or until hot.

1 Serving: Calories 250; Fat 12g; Cholesterol 60mg; Sodium 690mg; Carbohydrate 12g (Dietary Fiber 2g); Protein 25g.

Come and Eat!

Check out the selection of frozen appetizers such as egg rolls or pot-stickers at the supermarket—they can turn ordinary dinners into special dinners.

Have a Minute?

Add toasty crunch with toasted wonton skins! Cut wonton skins into thin strips and bake at 350° for 5 to 7 minutes or until light golden brown. Top teach serving with whole or broken toasted wonton strips.

Cashew Chicken

4 servings, about 1 cup each

- ⅓ **cup chicken broth**
- 1 **tablespoon cornstarch**
- 3 **tablespoons soy sauce**
- ½ **teaspoon ground ginger**
- ½ **teaspoon red pepper sauce**
- 2 **tablespoons vegetable oil**
- 1 **pound boneless, skinless chicken breast halves, cut crosswise into ½-inch strips**
- 1 **large green bell pepper, cut into ¾-inch pieces**
- 1 **medium onion, sliced**
- 1 **can (8 ounces) sliced water chestnuts, drained**
- ⅔ **cup dry-roasted cashews**
- 2 **green onions, sliced**

1. Mix broth, cornstarch, soy sauce, ginger and pepper sauce.

2. Heat wok or 12-inch skillet over high heat. Add 1 tablespoon of the oil; rotate wok to coat side. Add chicken; stir-fry about 4 minutes or until no longer pink in center. Remove chicken from wok; keep warm.

3. Add remaining 1 tablespoon oil to wok; rotate wok to coat side. Add bell pepper, onion and water chestnuts; stir-fry 2 minutes. Add cornstarch mixture to wok. Cook and stir about 1 minute or until sauce thickens. Stir in chicken and cashews. Garnish with green onions.

1 Serving: Calories 375; Fat 21g; Cholesterol 60mg; Sodium 1050mg; Carbohydrate 20g (Dietary Fiber 3g); Protein 30g.

Quick Jambalaya

4 servings

2 teaspoons vegetable oil

$\frac{1}{2}$ pound skinless, boneless chicken thighs, cut into $\frac{3}{4}$-inch cubes

$\frac{1}{2}$ pound fully cooked reduced-fat turkey kielbasa sausage, cut into $\frac{1}{4}$-inch slices

1 medium onion, sliced

1 medium green bell pepper, coarsely chopped

1 medium stalk celery, sliced

1 cup water

1 tablespoon all-purpose flour

1 can ($14\frac{1}{2}$ ounces) no-salt-added whole tomatoes, undrained

2 tablespoons steak sauce

$\frac{1}{4}$ to $\frac{1}{2}$ teaspoon red pepper sauce

2 cups cooked brown or white rice

1. Heat oil in nonstick Dutch oven over medium heat. Cook chicken in oil 8 to 10 minutes, stirring occasionally, until light brown. Stir in sausage, onion, bell pepper and celery. Cook, stirring frequently, until vegetables are crisp-tender.

2. Mix water and flour; stir into chicken mixture. Cook, stirring frequently, until slightly thickened.

3. Stir in tomatoes, steak sauce and pepper sauce, breaking up tomatoes. Heat to boiling; reduce heat. Simmer uncovered 10 to 15 minutes. Stir in rice; heat through.

1 Serving: Calories 330; Fat 11g; Cholesterol 80mg; Sodium 1000mg; Carbohydrate 34g (Dietary Fiber 4g); Protein 28g.